A Note to Parents and Teachers

SAINSBURY'S READING SCHEME is a compelling new reading programme for children, designed in conjunction with leading literacy experts, including Cliff Moon M.Ed., Honorary Fellow of the University of Reading. Cliff Moon has spent many years as a teacher and teacher educator specializing in reading and has written more than 140 books for children and teachers. He reviews regularly for teachers' journals.

Beautiful illustrations and superb full-colour photographs combine with engaging, easy-to-read stories to offer a fresh approach to each subject. Each book in the SAINSBURY'S READING SCHEME programme is guaranteed to capture a child's interest while developing his or her reading skills, general knowledge, and love of reading.

The five levels of the programme are aimed at different reading abilities, enabling you to choose the books that are exactly right for your child:

Yellow Level – Learning to read
Green Level – Beginning to read
Gold Level – Beginning to read alone
Ruby Level – Reading alone
Sapphire Level – Proficient readers

The "normal" age at which a child begins to read can be anywhere from three to eight years old, so these levels are only a general guideline.

No matter which level you select, you can be sure that you are helping your child learn to read, then read to learn!

KINGFISHER

First published 2012 by Kingfisher
an imprint of Macmillan Children's Books
a division of Macmillan Publishers Limited
20 New Wharf Road, London N1 9RR
Basingstoke and Oxford
Associated companies throughout the world
www.panmacmillan.com

Series editor: Heather Morris
Literacy consultant: Hilary Horton

ISBN: 978-0-7534-3828-2
Copyright © Macmillan Publishers Ltd 2012

All rights reserved. No part of this publication may
be reproduced, stored in or introduced into a retrieval
system, or transmitted, in any form or by any means
(electronic, mechanical, photocopying, recording or
otherwise), without the prior written permission of
the publisher. Any person who does any unauthorized
act in relation to this publication may be liable to
criminal prosecution and civil claims for damages.

9 8 7 6 5 4 3 2 1

1TR/0714/WKT/UG/105MA

A CIP catalogue record for this book is available from
the British Library.

Printed in China

This book is sold subject to the condition that it shall not,
by way of trade or otherwise, be lent, resold, hired out, or
otherwise circulated without the publisher's prior consent
in any form of binding or cover other than that in which it
is published and without a similar condition including this
condition being imposed on the subsequent purchaser.

Picture credits
The Publisher would like to thank the following for permission to reproduce their material.
Every care has been taken to trace copyright holders. However, if there have been unintentional
omissions or failure to trace copyright holders, we apologize and will, if informed, endeavour
to make corrections in any future edition.
(t = top, b = bottom, c = centre, r = right, l = left): Cover Shutterstock/Ian Stewart, Shutterstock/sculpies;
Pages 1 Shutterstock/Roberto Piras; 3 Shutterstock/tamaguramo; 5 Corbis/Robert Harding; 6 Corbis/Fridmar
Damm; 8 Corbis/Christine Osbourne; 11 Art Archive/Dagli Orti/Egyptian Museum Cairo; 12 Shutterstock/
sculpies; 13 Shutterstock/Ian Stewart; 16 Getty/De Agostini; 17 Shutterstock/RCH; 19 Margaret Maitland;
22 Art Archive/Dagli Orti; 23 Art Archive/Musée du Louvre/Dagli Orti; 27b Shutterstock/Vladimir Wrangel;
28 Art Archive/Musée du Louvre/Dagli Orti; 34 Shutterstock/RCH; 35 Corbis/Aladin Abdel Naby/Reuters;
36cl Shutterstock/maeadv; 36b Corbis/Ben Curtis/epa; 37bl Corbis/Sandro Vannini;
37br Shutterstock/tamaguramo; 38 Werner Forman Archive/British Museum; 39cr Art Archive/
Egyptian Museum Cairo/Kharbine-Tapabor/Boistesselin; 40 Corbis/Roger Wood; 41 Art Archive/
Gianni Dagli Orti; 42 Art Archive/Egyptian Museum Cairo/Dali Orti; 43 Corbis/Otto Lang;
44 AKG/Egyptian Museum Cairo; 45 Corbis/Bettman

Sainsbury's Reading Scheme

Sapphire Level Proficient readers

Ancient Egyptians

Written by Chris Oxlade

KINGFISHER

Opening the tomb

In ancient Egypt there was a secret valley. It was hidden among rocks and cliffs on the edge of the desert. It was a burial place for the **pharaohs**, the rulers of ancient Egypt. Today it is known as the Valley of the Kings.

In 1922 an **archaeologist** was looking for tombs in the valley. His name was Howard Carter. One day, he found a hidden door, buried by stones and earth.

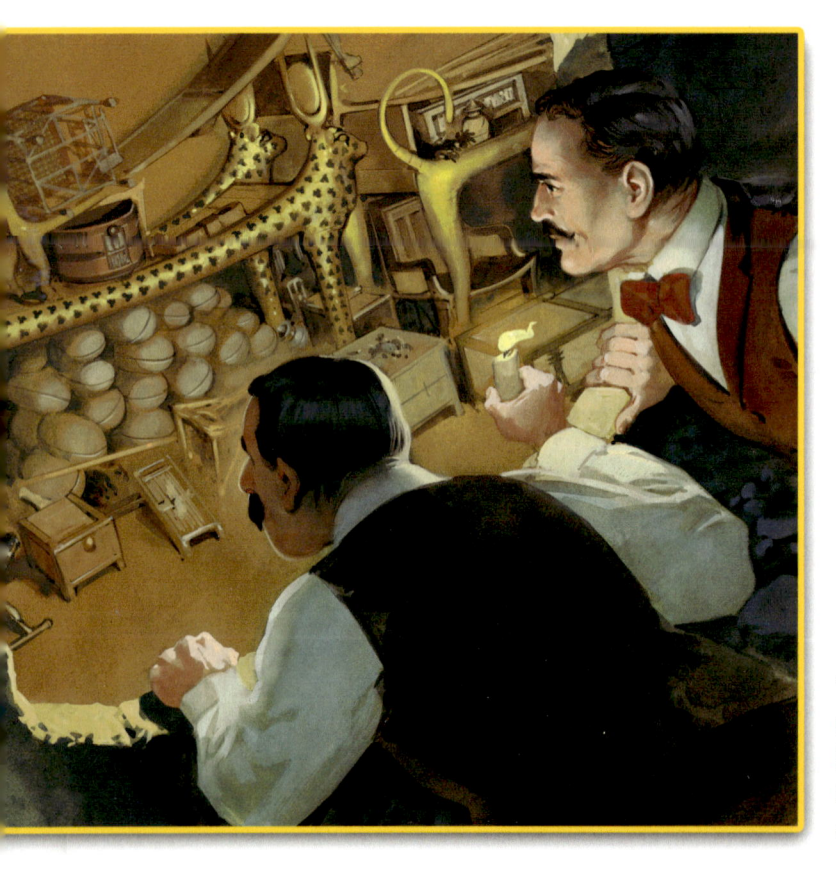

Tutankhamun's treasure had been buried for thousands of years.

This fine jewellery was made of gold and coloured glass.

Carter broke open the door and peered inside. He could see a gleam of gold. The tomb was filled with piles of treasure! There was jewellery, **ivory**, weapons, royal thrones and statues. The tomb belonged to a pharaoh called Tutankhamun, who died in 1324BCE. People all over the world were amazed at Howard Carter's discovery and the treasure of Tutankhamun.

Teenage king
Tutankhamun was not a very important king. He died when he was a teenager. Even so, his body was placed in a splendid coffin of gold.

The mighty Nile

If you fly over Egypt in a plane, you see great sandy deserts. The land is hot and dry and only a narrow green strip marks the course of a big river, called the Nile.

Boats still sail up and down the River Nile today.

The Nile carries rainwater from central Africa all the way to the Mediterranean Sea. Before the river reaches the coast it splits into many separate streams. This region of Egypt is called the Nile **delta**.

In ancient times, the river flooded every summer. The floods left behind thick black mud. This soil was very good for growing crops, which was why farmers first settled along the banks of the river thousands of years ago.

People used the river for watering their fields. It also gave them water to drink. They made boats from reeds or wood to travel up and down the river. Without the Nile, the ancient Egyptians could not have survived.

The Nile is about 6,670 kilometres long.
It is the longest river in the world.

Gods and goddesses

The Egyptians believed in many different gods and goddesses. Some of them were a part of nature or were linked with wild animals or birds. Painters showed the gods in pictures with horns or beaks, or the heads of animals.

Ra was the sun god. A god called Anubis was responsible for **mummies**. Osiris was the god of the dead and his wife Isis was the mother goddess. Horus was the god who looked after Egypt and its pharaohs.

People believed that the eye of Horus had healing powers.

How many gods?

There were at least 740 Egyptian gods and goddesses. One pharaoh called Akhenaten believed that there was just one god, called Aten, the disc of the sun. His ideas did not last. His son, Tutankhamun, went back to worshipping all the old gods.

Ra Osiris Isis Horus Anubis

The Egyptians believed that the pharaohs belonged to the family of the gods. They also believed that if the pharaohs did not do their duty the whole world could fall apart and there would be a state of **chaos**.

The kingdom of Egypt

The southern lands around the Nile were called Upper Egypt and the northern lands were called Lower Egypt. More than 5,000 years ago both regions became one country, ruled by a pharaoh.

Most pharaohs were men, but one woman, called Hatshepsut, did rule as pharaoh. Pharaohs wore crowns and headdresses and lived in grand palaces. The queen and royal family made up the **royal court** with the nobles. There were also many powerful officials, top priests and army leaders.

Other important people were doctors, engineers, **architects**, craft workers and priests.

Snake and bird

The badge of Lower Egypt was the cobra, a deadly snake. The badge of Upper Egypt was a bird called a vulture, which eats dead animals. The two became **symbols** of royal power.

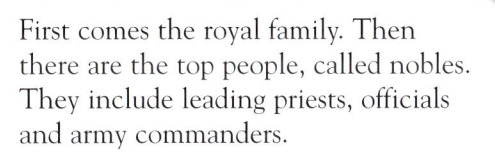

First comes the royal family. Then there are the top people, called nobles. They include leading priests, officials and army commanders.

In the third row are doctors, engineers, traders, **scribes** and architects.

The fourth row has minor priests and craft workers.

In the fifth row are soldiers, sailors, servants and performers.

At the bottom are labourers and slaves.

The big pyramids

Between June and September every year, the Nile flooded the fields. Labourers could not work on the land, so instead they had to help build temples or **monuments**.

Labourers built **pyramids** near the ancient city of Memphis on the orders of the pharaohs. These were like mountains made of stone blocks. One big pyramid, at a place called Saqqara, is more than 4,600 years old. It has four sides, with steps. A hundred years later the Egyptians built three pyramids at Giza which were even bigger and had smooth sides.

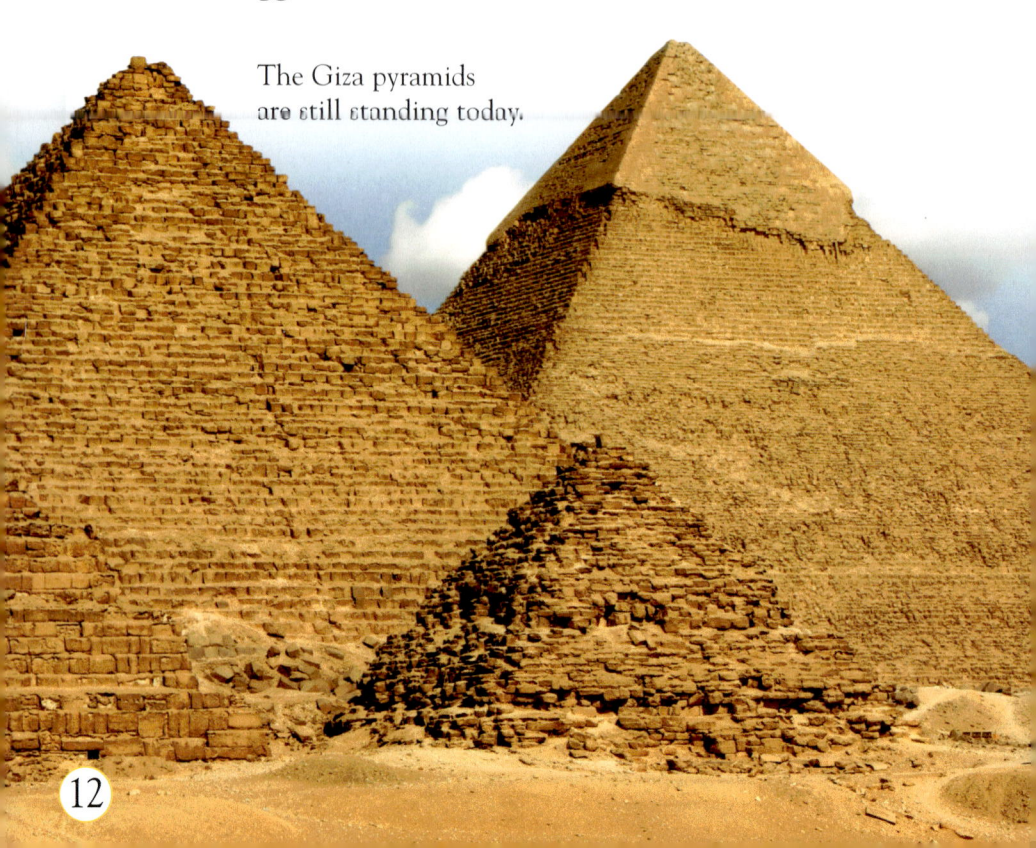

The Giza pyramids are still standing today.

A strange monster

Near the pyramids of Giza there is a giant, mysterious statue. It has the body of a lion and the face of a king. It is called the Great **Sphinx**.

Pyramids marked the tombs of dead pharaohs. The Egyptians believed that the spirit of the pharaoh went to the world of the gods, where he would live forever. They filled the tombs with treasures that the pharaoh could use in the next world.

Building at Giza

The biggest monument at Giza is the Great Pyramid. It is the tomb of a pharaoh called Khufu.

Building the Great Pyramid probably took thousands of workers more than 20 years. It was made from more than 2.3 million stone blocks, weighing between 2 and 15 tonnes each. The stone was cut from quarries and carried down the Nile in barges. Then labourers loaded it on to wooden **sleds** and dragged them over rollers to the site.

The builders probably built **ramps** from mud brick and soil to pull the stones up. Later they knocked the ramps away. Secret tunnels led to the burial chamber, sealed with massive stones. Even so, their treasures were stolen by robbers.

Wonder of the world
The Great Pyramid was 147 metres tall and it was the tallest building on Earth for thousands of years. Over time the wind and sand have worn it down and today it is 139 metres high.

15

Priests and temples

The ancient Egyptians built big stone temples. These had high gates, and courtyards with tall pillars. At the centre of each temple there was a holy **shrine**, with statues of the gods.

A pharaoh makes an offering to the god Atun.

Priests or priestesses offered food or drink to the gods. They burned **incense** and played music. They had to stay very clean and pure. Priests shaved their heads and washed at certain times of the day in a sacred pool. They could not wear wool or leather, or eat fish. Some special priests wore leopardskin robes.

Ordinary people could not enter temples to worship the gods. Sometimes there were big religious festivals when the priests took the statues of the gods out of the temples. They carried them in processions or up and down the river in boats.

Perfect place

Karnak was the biggest and most important religious site and the ancient Egyptians called it the Most Perfect Place. It was near the ancient city of Thebes and it took 1,300 years to build. There were three main temples and a sacred lake.

Ways of writing

Egyptian priests invented a way of writing made up of pictures and shapes. The symbols stood for sounds, ideas or things. We call these symbols **hieroglyphs**, which means sacred carvings. Hieroglyphs were carved on temples and monuments for thousands of years.

The Egyptians also invented other ways of writing. These flowing scripts were quicker to use. People used black or red ink, and pens made from reeds. Officials who could write were called scribes.

The Egyptians made a sort of paper from **papyrus**. This was a tall reed which grew by the river. The stalks were stripped, soaked and pressed together.

Hieroglyphic writing uses pictures of things like animals, plants, food, objects and buildings to make words and sentences.

People sometimes wrote quick notes or practised their handwriting on broken pottery.

After ancient Egyptian times, people forgot how to read the old writing. Then in 1799 some soldiers found a piece of stone at a place called Rosetta. It showed Egyptian scripts written next to ancient Greek words, which people still understood. About 20 years later people had worked out how to read hieroglyphs. This helped us to understand ancient Egypt.

Living in towns

The Egyptians built villages, towns and big cities such as Memphis and Thebes. Cities had walls to protect them from attack.

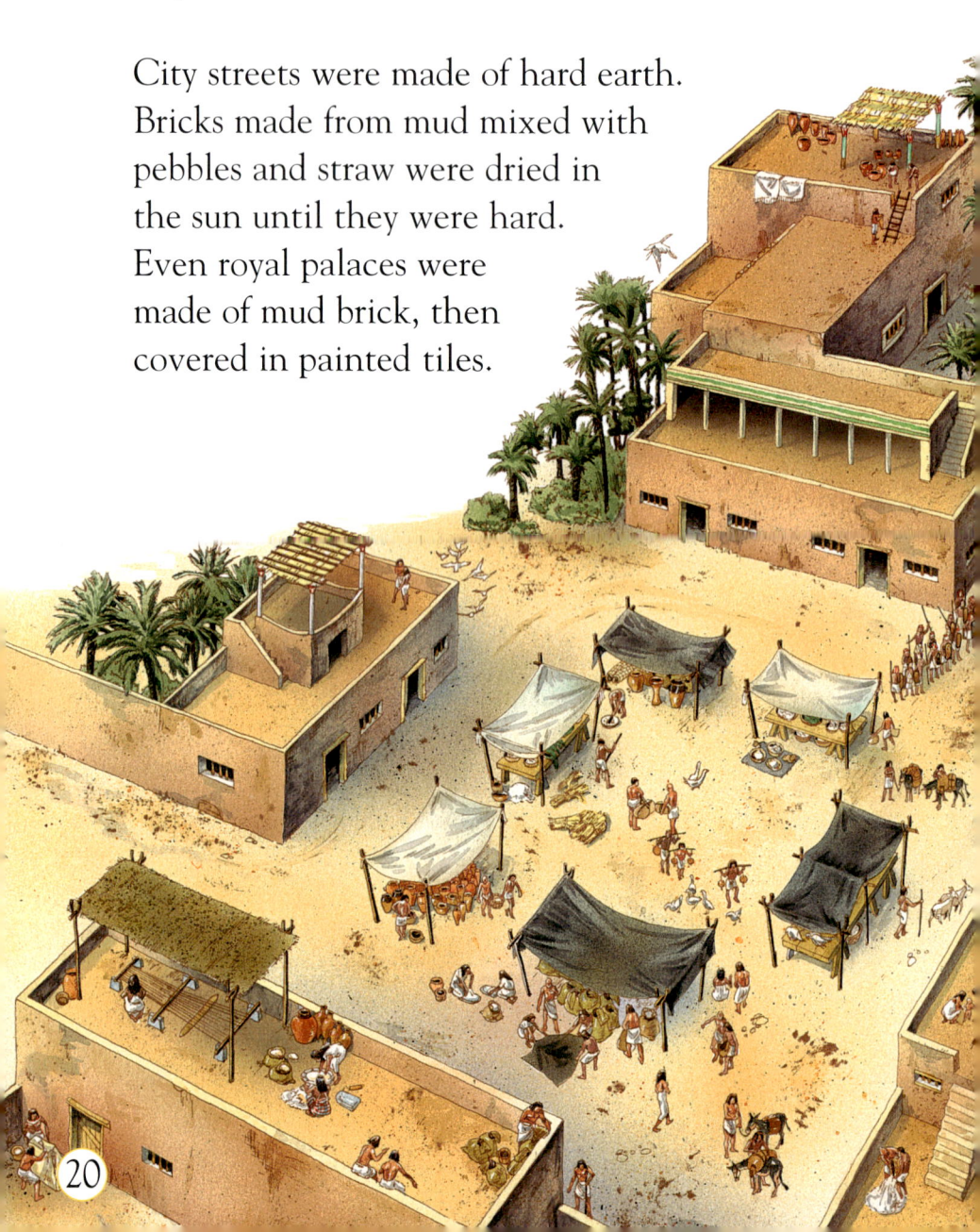

City streets were made of hard earth. Bricks made from mud mixed with pebbles and straw were dried in the sun until they were hard. Even royal palaces were made of mud brick, then covered in painted tiles.

During the day the streets were noisy. Markets were held in open squares between the houses. There were donkeys, children, and the hammering of metal workers, jewellers and furniture makers. Craft workers made pots, leather sandals and baskets.

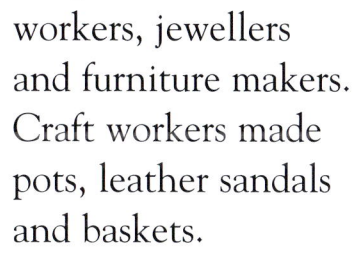

Some Egyptian houses had two or three floors, with beams made from palm tree trunks. People sat or slept on the flat roofs in the cool of the evening.

Going to the toilet
Egyptian toilet seats were often made of wood. They stood above a pottery jar filled with sand.

The farmer's year

Most Egyptians lived in villages in the delta or along the riverbanks. Farmers dug channels to bring water from the river through their fields. They also grew crops at **oases**, which were the few places in the desert where there was water.

Every November, oxen pulled ploughs over the soil. Farmers scattered seeds by hand. Herds of sheep or goats walked over them to push them into the ground.

A farmer ploughs his land. Dates are growing on the palm trees.

Women made bread from the grain grown and harvested by farmers.

Villagers used **sickles** made of wood and stone to harvest the wheat and barley. They made bread or beer from the grain. They grew vegetables such as peas, beans, cabbages, leeks and cucumbers. Dates, figs, grapes and melons were sweet and healthy food crops. When there was a poor crop people went hungry.

Farmers kept ducks, geese, pigs, goats and cattle to eat, and raised sheep for their wool.

Hippo havoc!
In some areas, hippopotamuses came out of the river at night and made a mess of the crops on the banks.

Food and feasts

Egyptian workers were paid with food instead of money. They stored food in pottery jars, and cooked in a clay oven. At a simple meal they might eat onions, beans, salted fish or fruit. The bread must have been a bit gritty because the teeth of ancient Egyptians were often worn down.

Nobles enjoyed hunting. Sometimes they brought home wild duck from the river or a deer from the desert, to serve at a feast. Beef stews or roast goose might be on the pharaoh's table, along with vegetables cooked in milk and cheese, tender figs, **pomegranates** and delicious honey cakes. The Egyptians drank red or white wine.

The nobles of the royal court loved grand **banquets**. They wore their finest clothes and jewellery. During and after the meal the guests watched musicians, acrobats and dancers putting on a show.

Sweet pastries
Sticky cakes and buns came in all shapes and sizes. Some were like doughnuts, while others were shaped as triangles or spirals. Some bakers made cakes in the shape of crocodiles.

25

Fashion and beauty

How do you keep cool in a hot country? The Egyptians wore light, loose clothes, made of plain white linen. Women wore a long dress, with shoulder straps. Men wore a tunic or just a **kilt**, a length of cloth worn around the waist like a skirt. Their clothes were sometimes decorated with pleats or folds.

Most people in the royal court wore clothes made of white linen.

A false beard
Pharaohs always wore a crown or headdress. No one was allowed to see their hair. At important events they wore a false beard as a symbol of being king.

Labourers and servants wore **loincloths**. Poor people made sandals from papyrus or grass, while rich people wore leather sandals. Children often ran around naked.

Nobles wore beautiful jewellery and broad collars made of beads. Both men and women wore make-up. The Egyptians made black eyeliner from a type of lead and lipstick from **ochre**, a red earth. They loved perfumes and scented oils.

Boys had shaved heads and a side lock of hair. Many men shaved their heads too, and both men and women often wore wigs.

Nefertiti was a powerful and beautiful queen. Look at her headdress, collar and make-up.

Everyday life

Children played with rattles, balls, spinning tops and toy lions and crocodiles. They wrestled and swam.

Most children had to work when they were quite small. Boys helped in the fields, or learned skills in their father's workshop. Girls learned how to weave cloth and cook.

Children from important families, especially boys, learned reading, writing and sums. They were beaten if they made mistakes.

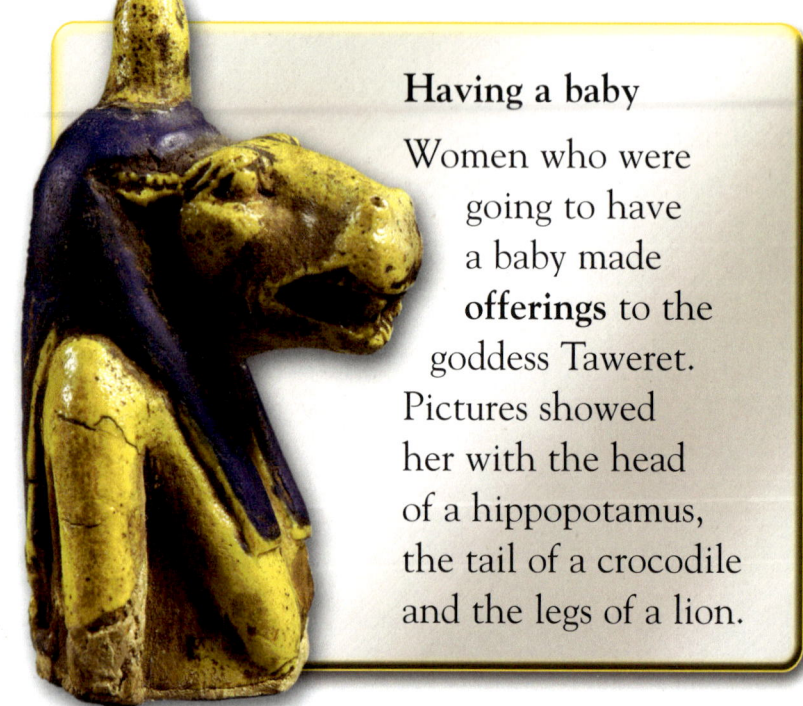

Having a baby

Women who were going to have a baby made **offerings** to the goddess Taweret. Pictures showed her with the head of a hippopotamus, the tail of a crocodile and the legs of a lion.

Women married before the age of 15 and men by the time they were 20. Marriages were arranged by the parents, although love did play a part in choosing a husband or wife.

Poor people often died by the time they were 30 or 40, but rich people might live to be 70 or older. One pharaoh, Ramesses II, was about 90 when he died.

Making mummies

Egyptians believed that after they died they would be with the gods forever. They wanted their bodies to be turned into mummies. This made sure that the bodies kept their shape and could travel safely to the world of the gods.

To make a mummy, the priests first cleaned the body. Then they pulled the brain out through the nose, using a hook. They cut out the guts, liver, lungs and stomach, dried them and put them in jars.

They dried the body for 40 days in a kind of salt called **natron**.

Then they stuffed the body with linen cloth or sawdust. It was covered in gum and oil and wrapped in linen bandages, with lucky charms. They put a mask over the head.

Ancient mummies are still being discovered today. Archaeologists study them carefully. They can find out from mummies what people ate and how they lived and worked.

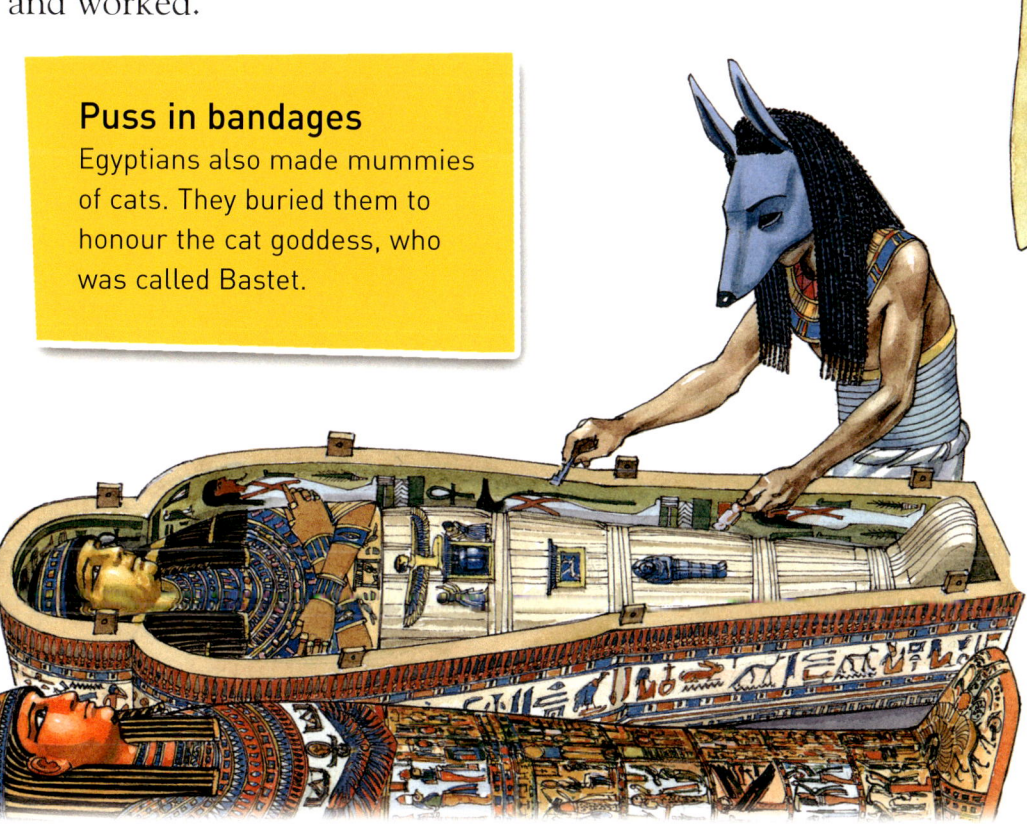

Puss in bandages
Egyptians also made mummies of cats. They buried them to honour the cat goddess, who was called Bastet.

A funeral procession

The mummy makers placed the body inside a wooden coffin in the shape of a human body. They painted the wood to look like the person who had died.

Royal mummies might have several coffin cases, one inside the other. A large stone chest called a **sarcophagus** held the coffins in the tomb.

At the funeral procession, long lines of women wept and wailed. Priests made offerings to the gods, sprinkling milk and burning sweet incense. The coffin was hauled to the burial ground by oxen on a sled shaped like a boat.

In this boat the dead pharaoh travelled to meet the god Osiris, who ruled the world of the dead.

Priests carried out one last **ceremony**, to make sure that the pharaoh could come back to life in the next world. They called this Opening the Mouth. Then they placed the body in its tomb.

A dead pharaoh is taken to his tomb.

Food for the dead
There were stone tables near the entrance to the tomb. People left food and drink there, to feed the mummy's spirit.

Raiders and robbers

Pharaohs stopped marking their tombs with pyramids and began hiding them underground because robbers kept breaking in to steal the treasure.

At first the Valley of the Kings seemed the perfect place for royal burials, because it was hidden in cliffs on the edge of the desert west of Thebes, and the valley could be easily guarded.

The Valley of the Kings was used between about 3,500 and 3,000 years ago.

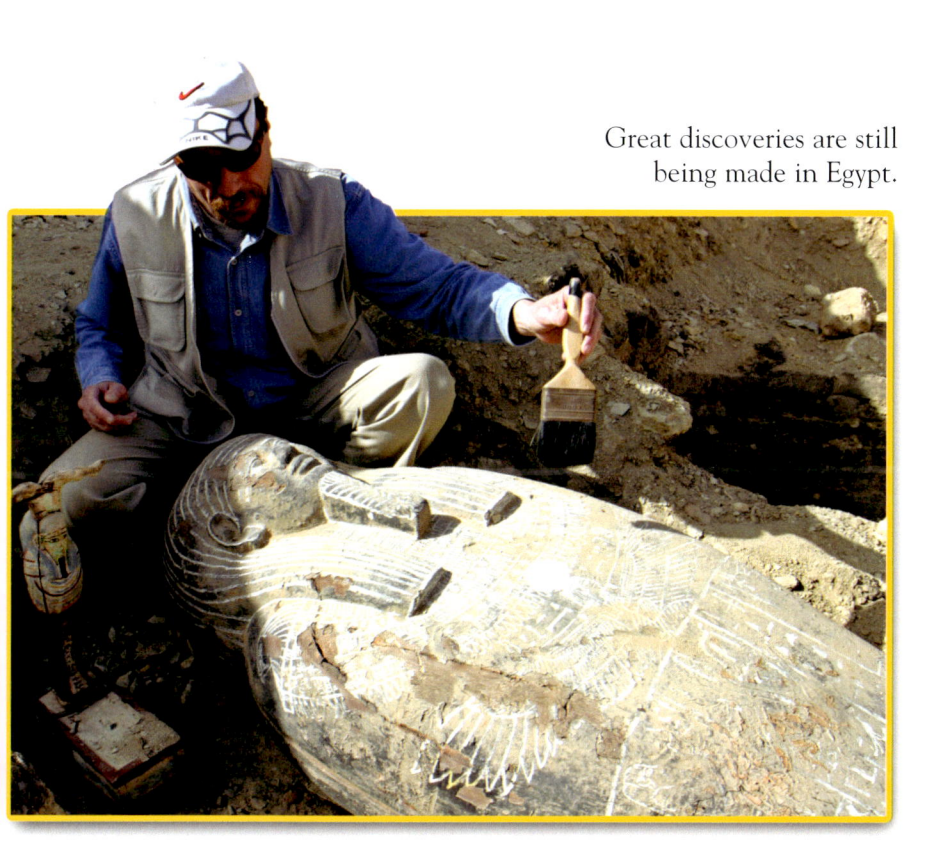

Great discoveries are still being made in Egypt.

The tombs were full of dead-ends and deadly drops, to stop the robbers reaching the royal treasure. Even so, robbers broke into many tombs.

Archaeologists have found 63 tombs or burial places in the Valley of the Kings. Nearby there is also a Valley of the Queens and a Valley of the Nobles. Wall paintings in many of them tell us about life in ancient Egypt, but most of the treasure disappeared thousands of years ago.

Death to robbers!
Anyone who robbed a pharaoh's tomb faced a terrible punishment. They could be stuck on a pointed wooden stake!

Treasures of Tutankhamun

The most famous tomb ever found in Egypt belonged to the young pharaoh Tutankhamun. His tomb was smaller than others, but because robbers had not taken away all the treasures, it was packed with beautiful things. Archaeologists think that robbers did try to break into the tomb, but may have been disturbed.

Howard Carter, the man who discovered the tomb, spent years working on it, clearing passages and chambers and making lists of all the wonderful things he found. There were chariot wheels and trumpets, daggers, bows and arrows, painted chests and golden thrones.

A beautiful ring found in Tutankhamun's tomb and his golden mask.

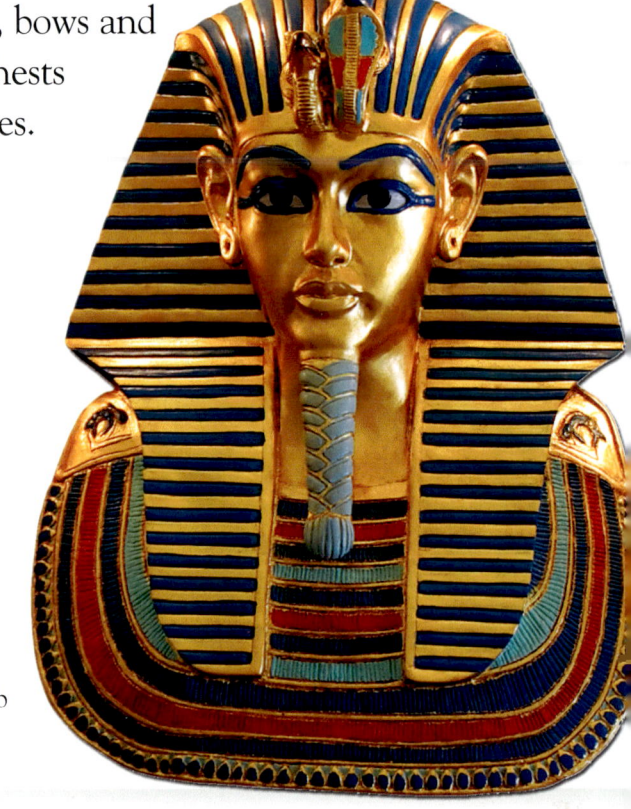

How did he die?

Tutankhamun's remains have been scanned and X-rayed several times in recent years. Some archaeologists claim the young king was murdered. Others believe he had an accident, hitting his head and breaking his leg. Some think he died of a fever after the accident.

Tutankhamun is taken away for an X-ray.

Carved wooden animals, cups, beds and stools lay beside board games, jewels, fans and golden sandals. There were even boxes of food, for the pharaoh to eat on his journey to the world of the dead.

In 1925 Howard Carter opened the inner coffin and gazed at last on the mummy of Tutankhamun. Over the face was a mask of solid gold and a blue stone called **lapis lazuli**.

Traders and explorers

The Egyptians did not use money or metal coins in the time of the pharaohs. They exchanged goods or services. This way of swapping things is called **barter**. In the market they swapped grain for pots and jars, or jewellery for a knife.

At market, the Egyptians used scales to weigh goods ready to barter.

The Egyptians sometimes used rings of copper, silver or gold in their exchanges. They might swap a bed worth 20 units of copper for a wooden chest of the same value.

The pharaohs exchanged precious gifts with the rulers of other countries. The Egyptians built sailing ships and traded with other peoples who lived around the Mediterranean Sea and Arabia. Egyptian explorers sailed down the Red Sea to a land they called Punt. This was probably somewhere in East Africa. They brought back ivory, precious woods, incense and wild animals such as pet monkeys and sacred baboons.

Long-distance trade

Traders brought the valuable blue gemstone known as lapis lazuli all the way from Afghanistan to Egypt – about 4,000 kilometres.

Lapis lazuli bracelet

Egyptian ships arrive in Punt.

Egypt at war

The Egyptians believed that their pharaohs should rule all the lands created by the gods. Pictures show the pharaohs crushing Egypt's enemies. Egyptian soldiers fought against Nubia, the African country to the south. Their armies marched west into Libya and east into Asia. The pharaoh Ramesses II fought a great battle at Qadesh, against a people called the Hittites.

An Egyptian army goes to war. These models were found in an ancient tomb.

Ramesses II in his chariot at the Battle of Qadesh.

The Egyptians built strong forts from mud bricks. Soldiers were called up to take part in battles or expeditions and slaves could win their freedom by fighting in the army. They fought with bows and arrows, swords, axes and spears, and carried shields and clubs called **maces**. They hurled stones at the enemy with **slings**. The first metal weapons were copper. Later ones were made of bronze and iron.

Egyptian armies began to use chariots pulled by horses about 3,500 years ago. Archers stood on them to fire arrows at the enemy.

Victory!
In 1456BCE a pharaoh called Thutmose III fought a battle for the city of Megiddo. The Egyptians captured 2,000 horses and 924 chariots.

41

After the pharaohs

In the end, the Egyptian pharaohs lost their power over Egypt. Other peoples came to rule the lands around the River Nile, including the Persians, Greeks, Romans, Arabs and Turks.

New cities were built. The port of Alexandria became a great centre of learning. Cairo became the biggest city in Africa, but the world forgot the old ways of life in Egypt. Sand covered the ruined monuments. During the 1700s and 1800s, Europeans became interested in ancient Egypt. They carried away monuments and treasures to their own countries.

Then archaeologists began to work in a more scientific way. They took more care of ancient temples and tombs and built a new museum in Cairo.

The mayor of Thebes with his wife and daughter

Moving a temple

In the 1960s the Egyptians built a new **dam** at Aswan, which raised the water level of the River Nile. The Great Temple at Abu Simbel had to be taken apart and moved to higher ground, where it was rebuilt.

Today and forever

Egyptian archaeologists are still searching for ancient remains. In 2009 they found 30 mummies inside one tomb at Saqqara. They had been there for 2,600 years.

Today visitors come to Egypt from all over the world. They travel up the River Nile and explore the ancient pyramids, temples and tombs. Tutankhamun is the most famous pharaoh still lying in the Valley of the Kings. He is more famous today than he was in his own lifetime.

A beautiful cup was found in Tutankhamun's tomb. On it were the words:

May your spirit live on,
May you spend millions of years, you who love Thebes,
With your face to the wind from the north
And your eyes seeing happiness.

Ancient Egypt key dates

BCE

c6000	Farmers grow crops around the Nile.
c3400	Walled towns are built in Egypt.
c3100	Egypt is ruled as one kingdom.
c2650	The stepped pyramid is built at Saqqara.
c2560	The Great Pyramid is built at Giza.
c2500	The Great Sphinx is built at Giza.
c1550	Burials take place in the Valley of the Kings, near Thebes.
1483	Queen Hatshepsut dies.
1478	The Battle of Megiddo ends with a victory for Thutmose III.
1379	The pharaoh Akhenaten brings in sun worship.
1324	The pharaoh Tutankhamun dies.
1274	The Battle of Qadesh is fought by Ramesses II.
525	The Persians rule Egypt.

Glossary

archaeologist Someone who studies ancient remains and ruins.

architect Someone who designs buildings.

banquet A feast for many guests.

barter To swap one thing for another, instead of buying or selling it for money.

BCE Before the Common Era (any date before 1CE). It is also sometimes known as BC.

ceremony A public action carried out by priests or officials.

chaos Complete disorder and confusion.

dam A wall built across a river to control its flow.

delta A coastal area where a build-up of mud forces a river to split into separate streams.

hieroglyph Picture writing used in ancient Egypt.

incense Wood or gum which smells sweet when burned.

ivory Elephants' tusks.

kilt A length of cloth worn around the waist, like a skirt.

lapis lazuli A blue gemstone.

loincloth A short piece of cloth tied around the waist.

mace A club-like weapon.

monument A large statue or pillar in a public place.

mummy A dead body which has been dried and prepared so it does not rot.

natron A sort of salt.

oasis A waterhole in the desert, where plants can grow.

ochre A sort of earth, coloured red, brown or yellow.

offering Food, drink or other objects offered to a god or goddess.

papyrus A sort of paper made from reeds.

pharaoh A ruler of ancient Egypt.

pomegranate A sort of fruit grown in warm countries.

pyramid A four-sided stone monument with a square base and triangular sides rising to a point.

ramp A slope of soil or rock.

royal court The people around a ruler, including the royal family, nobles and officials.

sarcophagus A stone chest made to hold a coffin.

scribe Someone whose job is to copy writing or make notes, an official in ancient Egypt.

shrine A holy place built to honour a god.

sickle A curved cutting blade, used to harvest crops.

sled A large wooden board used for transporting heavy loads.

sling A strap used for hurling stones at an enemy.

sphinx A statue with the body of a lion and the head of a human.

symbol One thing that stands for another.

Index

boats 6, 7, 14, 17, 32, 33, 38, 39

Cairo 42
Carter, Howard 4, 5, 36, 37
coffins 5, 32, 37

Giza 7, 12, 13, 14–15, 45
gods and goddesses 8–9, 16, 17, 28, 31, 32, 33
  Anubis 8, 9
  Aten (or Atun) 9, 16
  Bastet 31
  Horus 8, 9
  Isis 8, 9
  Osiris 8, 9, 33
  Ra 8, 9
  Taweret 28

hieroglyphs 18–19, 46

jewellery 5, 21, 24, 27, 36, 37, 38, 39

mummies 30–31, 32, 33, 37, 44, 46

Nefertiti, Queen 27
Nile
  delta 6, 7, 22, 46
  river 6–7, 10, 12, 14, 42, 43, 44, 45

papyrus 18, 27, 47
pharaohs 4, 9, 10, 13, 14, 27, 29, 33, 34, 35, 36, 37, 38, 40, 41, 42, 44, 45, 47
  Akhenaten 9, 45
  Hatshepsut 10, 45
  Khufu 14
  Ramesses II 29, 40, 41, 45
  Thutmose III 41, 45
  Tutankhamun 4–5, 9, 36–37, 44, 45
priests 10, 11, 16–17, 18, 30, 32, 33
pyramids 12–13, 14, 34, 44, 47

robbers 14, 34–35, 36
Rosetta stone 19

Saqqara 12, 44, 45
sphinxes 13, 45, 47

Thebes 7, 17, 20, 34, 42, 44, 45
tombs 4–5, 13, 14, 32, 33, 34, 35, 36–37, 40, 42, 44

Valley of the Kings 4–5, 34–35, 44, 45

weapons 5, 36, 41

Sainsbury's
Reading Scheme

CERTIFICATE
of Reading

My name is

_____

I have read

_____

Date

_____